GALE
CENGAGE Learning

Novels for Students, Volume 2

Copyright © 1997

Gale Research
835 Penobscot Building
645 Griswold St.
Detroit, Ml 48226-4094

This book is printed on acid-free paper that meets the minimum requirements of American National Standard for Information Sciences—Permanence Paper for Printed Library Materials, ANSI Z39.48-1984.

ISBN 0-7876-1687-7
ISSN 1094-3552

Printed in the United States of America
10 9 8 7 6 5 4

Invisible Man

Ralph Ellison

1952

Introduction

At its appearance in 1952, *Invisible Man* was immediately hailed as a masterpiece. A work both epic and richly comic, it won the National Book Award for its author, Ralph Ellison. *Invisible Man* has been translated into fourteen languages and has never been out of print. A 1965 Book Week poll of two hundred writers and critics selected it as the most distinguished novel of the previous twenty years. Written in the style of a *bildungsroman*, or novel of education, the book chronicles the sometimes absurd adventures of a young black man whose successful search for identity ends with the realization that he is invisible to the white world. *Invisible Man* is structurally complex and densely symbolic; some critics, in fact, faulted it for what they saw as literary excess. A major controversy centered on the book's intended audience: some black critics argued that it was or should have been a "race" novel, while white critics were relieved that it was not. It also aroused the ire of black nationalists for sacrificing the broader concerns of black nationhood in the defense of a narrow individualism. This contentiousness dissipated over time, however, and the novel's enduring qualities are now undisputed. *Invisible Man* deals with themes of individuality, identity, history, and responsibility. The protagonist is repeatedly exhorted to look beneath the surface of things. Although Ellison freely acknowledged his debt to both European and African American literary traditions, he used an astonishing range of African American folk forms in constructing his protagonist's universe. Critics agree that the influence of *Invisible Man* on American literature in general, and its role in bringing the blues and folklore into the mainstream of black experience in particular, is incalculable.

As a boy, Ralph Waldo Ellison announced that his ambition was to become a Renaissance man. "I was taken very early," he would write, "with a passion to link together all I loved within the Negro community and all those things I felt in the world which lay beyond." Ellison was born on March 1, 1914, in Oklahoma City, Oklahoma, to Ida Millsap and Lewis Ellison, who died when Ralph was three. Ellison's mother worked tirelessly to provide a stimulating environment for Ralph and his brother, and her influence on the writer was profound.

In 1933, at the age of nineteen, Ellison hopped a freight train to Tuskegee Institute in Macon County, Alabama, where he majored in music. In the summer of 1935 he traveled north to New York City to earn money for his last year in college; he never returned to Tuskegee. Instead, he stayed in New York and worked for a year as a freelance photographer, file clerk, and builder and seller of hi-fi systems, still intending a career in music. But then Richard Wright, the noted author of *Black Boy* and *Native Son*, invited him to write a book review for the 1937 issue of *New Challenge*, and Ellison's career was decided.

In 1938 Ellison joined the Federal Writers Project, which gave him opportunities to do research and to write, and helped to build his appreciation of folklore. Like other black intellectuals in the 1930s, he found the Communist party's active antiracist stance appealing, but Ellison was also a fervent individualist, and he never became a party member. During 1942 Ellison was managing editor of the *Negro Quarterly*, but thereafter he turned to writing stories. Two of his most acclaimed stories before the publication of *Invisible Man* were "Flying Home" (1944) and "King of the Bingo Game" (1944); both dealt with questions of identity. Ellison met Fanny McConnell in 1944, and the couple married in 1946.

During World War II Ellison served as a cook in the merchant marines. He returned to the United States in 1945 and began *Invisible Man.* The novel appeared in 1952 and was a commercial and critical success, winning the National Book Award in 1953, although some black nationalists felt the novel was not political enough. Ellison continued to write short stories, and in 1964 he published *Shadow and Act*, a collection of essays and interviews about the meaning of experience. Many awards and lecture and teaching engagements followed, both at home and abroad, and Ellison became regarded as an expert on African American culture and folklore, American studies, and creative writing.

The major question of Ellison's later life was whether and when he would publish another novel. He had reportedly been working on a book since 1955, but his progress was slow, and in 1967 a fire at Ellison's home destroyed about 350 pages of the manuscript. The novel was left unfinished at his death, although eight excerpts from it have been published in literary journals. In 1986 Ellison published *Going to the Territory*, a collection of previously published speeches, reviews, and essays. He died of pancreatic cancer on April 16, 1994.

Plot Summary

Prologue

Ralph Ellison's *Invisible Man* chronicles the life of an unnamed, first-person narrator from his youth in the segregated American South of the 1920s to a temporary "hibernation," twenty years later, in a "border area" of Harlem. From his "hole in the ground," this "invisible man" responds to his "compulsion to put invisibility down in black and white" by telling his story. He begins by attempting to explain his own invisibility: "I am invisible, understand, simply because people refuse to see me." The tendency of others to distort what they see or to see "everything and anything" except him leads the narrator to question his own existence. As a result, he feels resentment toward those who refuse to acknowledge his reality. When he bumps into one such person on the street, the narrator responds to the man's slurs with swift violence. He is kept from killing him only by the unnerving realization that his victim did not, in fact, *see* him as another human being but rather as a "phantom" or a mirage. The narrator notes one curious advantage of invisibility, a "slightly different sense of time" that allows one to "see around corners." After accidentally smoking a "reefer" and experiencing a hallucinogenic journey back through history to slave times, the narrator recognizes that his awareness of invisibility alone gives him a more useful sense of sight. He has, as he puts it, "illuminated the blackness of my invisibility," and it remains for him to explain, in the rest of the novel, what has brought him to this newfound understanding of his own identity and of his role in American society.

Chapters 1-6

The narrator begins his story with his memories of youth and adolescence in a small southern town. He recalls first, as the most baffling but powerful memory of his childhood, the final instructions of his dying grandfather that he must live as a "traitor" and "a spy in the enemy's territory." These words become "like a curse" to the narrator as he grows older, for he finds reward in living a life of outward humility and he doesn't understand how such a life might be called "treachery." Asked by the leading white citizens of the town to repeat his graduation speech extolling submissiveness, the narrator finds himself required to participate in a battle royal, a blindfolded boxing match with nine of his schoolmates. Bloodied from the fight and humiliated by the racist jeers of the white men, the narrator still delivers his speech about "social responsibility" and receives, as a "badge of office," a brief case and a college scholarship.

The narrator's education at the "state college for Negroes" comes to an abrupt end during his junior year, when he shows a wealthy white benefactor of the college, Mr. Norton, parts of the South that the college wishes to hide from its Northern visitors. Mr. Norton is horrified by what he hears from Jim Trueblood (a black sharecropper who has impregnated his own daughter) and by what he sees in the Golden Day (a "slave-quarter" brothel). Because he has thus embarrassed the school and threatened its reputation, the narrator is temporarily expelled by the president of the college, Dr. Bledsoe. After listening to an impassioned speech about the school's mission by Homer A. Barbee, the narrator is advised by Bledsoe to go to New York to earn his fees for the following year. Provided with sealed letters to several of the school's "friends" in the North, the narrator boards a bus, optimistic that he will soon return to complete his education.

Chapters 7-14

The narrator's confidence soon wavers, when a veteran from the Golden Day heading North on the same bus urges him to "come out of the fog" and "learn to look beneath the surface" of his life. Once in New York the narrator feels alternately confident and frightened, more free than in the South but more confused. His doubts increase after his first six letters yield no job opportunities. With his seventh letter the narrator meets Young Emerson, the disillusioned son of one of the college's wealthy benefactors, from whom he learns that Bledsoe's letters of introduction in fact bar him from ever returning to the school. Stunned by this discovery, the narrator abandons his loyalty and submission to the college and knows that he will "never be the same."

Finding work at the Liberty Paint factory, the narrator is branded a "fink" by the unionized workers, then moments later is accused of being a unionizer by Lucius Brockway. Before the end of the day he contributes to a boiler-room explosion that leaves him seriously injured and unconscious. He awakes in the factory hospital, where, in order to assure that "society will suffer no traumata on his account," doctors attempt to "cure" him with an electric-shock lobotomy. After his release from the hospital, the narrator is unsure of who he is, feeling disconnected from both his mind and his body. Drifting back to Harlem, he is taken in by Mary Rambo, an elderly black woman he meets coming out of the Lenox Avenue subway. Here his search for identity becomes an "obsession," and he roams the city without purpose until he comes across an eviction in progress. Speaking to the angry crowd in defense of the elderly black couple, the narrator comes to the attention of a member of the politically radical Brotherhood. Recruited as a spokesperson for their cause, the narrator accepts a new name and a "new identity" and resolves once again to "leave the old behind."

Chapters 15-25

After parting from Mary and moving into an apartment provided by the Brotherhood, the narrator delivers his first speech at a political rally. Encouraged by his own performance and the emotional reaction of the crowd, he resolves to find a meaningful identity in the Brotherhood that is "not limited by black and white." After the narrator meets Tod Clifton, another young black man active in the Brotherhood, the two are involved in a street fight with the black nationalist Ras the Exhorter. Although denounced by Ras for working side by side with white men, the narrator is "dominated by the all-embracing idea of Brotherhood" and convinced that he plays a "vital role" in the work of the organization. His confidence is momentarily shaken by an anonymous warning that he not "get too big," but he is reminded of what he is working for by Brother Tarp's gift of a leg link that he had filed open to escape from a southern chain gang.

The narrator begins to question the aims of the Brotherhood after he is denounced by Brother Wrestrum and is transferred out of Harlem to lecture downtown on "the Woman Question." When he returns to Harlem after Tod Clifton's disappearance, he finds the movement weakened and disorganized and discovers Clifton on the street hawking paper Samnbo dolls. Moments later, the narrator watches as Clifton is gunned down by a police officer. With his eyes opened to aspects of Harlem and of the Brotherhood that he had never seen before, the narrator leads a funeral march for Clifton at which he abandons "scientific" political arguments for honest emotional expression. Roaming the streets of Harlem after again being denounced by the Brotherhood, the narrator discovers a world of contradiction and "possibility" that causes him to see his past experiences in a new light:

> ... leaning against that stone wall in the sweltering night, I began to accept my past and, as I accepted it, I felt memories welling up within me. It was as though I'd learned suddenly to look around corners; images of past humiliations flickered through my head and I saw that they were more than separate experiences. They were me; they defined me. I was my experiences and my experiences were me, and no blind men, no matter how powerful they became, even if they conquered the world, could take that, or change one single itch, taunt, laugh, cry, scar, ache, rage or pain of it. They were blind, bat blind, moving only by the echoed sounds of their own voices. ... They were very much the same, each attempting to force his picture of reality upon me and neither giving a hoot in hell for how things looked to me. I was simply a material, a natural resource to be used. I had switched from the arrogant absurdity of Norton and Emerson to that of Jack and the Brotherhood, and it all came out the same—except I now recognized my invisibility.

After this powerful recognition, the narrator resolves to undermine the Brotherhood. But before he can discover their plans for him and for Harlem, he is swept up in a riot initiated by Ras, now called "the Destroyer." Narrowly escaping death at the hands of Ras and his henchmen, the narrator falls into an open manhole where he sleeps, dreams, and eventually decides to "take up residence."

Epilogue

From his "hole in the ground," the narrator ends his story by reflecting on his painful past, his present uncertainty and anger, and the possibility that he may yet emerge from his "hibernation" and —though still an invisible man in American society —find "a socially responsible role to play."

Characters

The Reverend Homer A. Barbee

A blind preacher from Chicago of substantial rhetorical skill who gives the Founder's Day speech at the college.

Dr. A. Herbert Bledsoe

Dr. Bledsoe is the president of the college attended by the invisible man. Called "Old Bucket-head" by the students, he is a shrewd survivor who has spent his career humoring the white trustees in the hopes of retaining his position. A person of considerable affectation, he can manage even in striped trousers and a swallow-tail coat topped by an ascot tie to make himself look humble. He is aghast when the invisible man tells him that he took Mr. Norton to see Jim Trueblood because that's what the trustee wanted to do: "My God, boy! You're black and living in the South—did you forget how to lie?" His recipe for success is to attain power and influence by making the right contacts and "then stay in the dark and use it!" His self-interest makes him capable of betrayal, as when he lets the invisible man head off for New York City thinking that the letters he is carrying addressed to various trustees are letters of recommendation.

Lucius Brockway

The invisible man's irascible second supervisor at Liberty Paints. "Lucius Brockway not only intends to protect hisself, he *knows how* to do it! Everybody knows I been here ever since there's been a here." His one worry is that the union will do him out of a job.

Brother Tod Clifton

Young and handsome, Clifton is the leader of the Brotherhood youth: "a hipster, a zoot suiter, a sharpie." He has run-ins with Ras the Exhorter over their philosophical differences. He is friendly and helpful to the invisible man, despite the hero's being made his superior. "I saw no signs of resentment," says the invisible man in admiration, "but a complete absorption in the strategy of the meeting. … I had no doubt that he knew his business." Brother Clifton has put his full faith in the brotherhood, and when he is abandoned by it, his despair is total. He plunges "outside of history," becoming a street peddler selling paper black sambo dolls, and is murdered by the police. His death is a defining moment for the invisible man.

Emma

One of the first members of the Brotherhood the invisible man meets. The hero is skeptical of the Brotherhood's motives when he hears Emma ask, "But don't you think he should be a little blacker?"

Media Adaptations

- *Invisible Man* was recorded by Dr. Marion J. Smith for Golden Voice Production, 1993.

Grandfather

The invisible man's grandfather, whom the protagonist had always thought of as a model of desirable conduct. He is dead when the novel begins, but his influence on the invisible man is powerful. His dying words were, "Son, ... I never told you, but our life is a war and I have been a traitor all my born days, a spy in the enemy's country ever since I give up my gun back in the Reconstruction. Live with your head in the lion's mouth. I want you to overcome 'em with yeses, undermine 'em with grins, agree 'em to death and destruction, let 'em swoller you till they vomit or bust wide open.... Learn it to the younguns." These words prick the invisible man's complacency, and he remembers them as a curse that haunts him throughout his journey, a reminder that all is not right in the world.

Halley

The spirited manager at The Golden Day.

Brother Hambro

Hambro takes the invisible man through a four-month period of intense study and indoctrination after his arena speech to the Brotherhood to correct his "unscientific" tendencies. "A tall, friendly man, a lawyer, and the Brotherhood's chief theoretician." he tells the invisible man that "it's impossible *not* to take advantage of the people....The trick is to take advantage of them in their own best interest."

Invisible Man

The unnamed protagonist of the novel. In explaining to the reader what he has done to be so "black and blue," the hero says, "I was looking for myself and asking everyone except myself questions which I, and only I, could answer." By the end of his adventures, he will conclude "that I am nobody but myself. But first I had to discover that I am an invisible man!" The invisible man starts his tale as an innocent, one who believes that "humility was the secret, indeed, the very essence of progress." His greatest aspiration is to be an assistant to Dr. Bledsoe, the president of his college, who kowtows to whites in an attempt to hold on to his position. The invisible man believes, consciously or unconsciously, "the great false wisdom ... that white is right" and that it is "advantageous to flatter rich white folks." He grudgingly admires other blacks who do not share his scruples; for instance, he is both humiliated and fascinated by the sharecropper Jim Trueblood's self-confessed tale of incest, and he is similarly impressed by the vet at The Golden Day: "I wanted to tell Mr. Norton that the man was crazy and yet I received a fearful satisfaction from hearing him talk as he had to a white man."

Although he has the "queer feeling that I was playing a part in some scheme which I did not understand," he ignores his instincts, as when, for instance, he personally delivers to prospective employers in New York City what he foolishly believes to be positive letters of recommendation from Dr. Bledsoe "like a hand of high trump cards." For every two steps forward, he takes one back. His experience in the factory hospital, for example, is a kind of awakening, and he develops an "obsession with my identity" that causes him to "put into words feelings which I had hitherto suppressed." But though he is skeptical of the Brotherhood's motives in recruiting him—"What am I, a man or a natural resource?"—and their obvious emphasis on the "we," the invisible man sets aside his misgivings and embraces the organization; "it was a different, bigger 'we,'" he tells himself. He is kind, joining the Brotherhood partly out of desire to pay Mary Rambo the rent money he owes her, and loyal to people like Brother Tarp and Brother Clifton in whom he senses a fundamental goodness. But he is forever second-guessing himself, and it takes the raw injustice of Brother Clifton's murder to spark the invisible man into consciousness: "Outside the Brotherhood we were outside history; but inside of it they didn't see us.... Now I recognized my invisibility." At first defiant—"But to whom can I be responsible, and why should I be, when you refuse to see me?"—by the end of the novel the invisible man is ready to come out, "since there's a possibility that even an invisible man has a socially responsible role to play."

Brother Jack

The Brotherhood's district leader for Harlem, he befriends the invisible man after hearing him address a crowd gathered to witness the eviction of an elderly black couple, and sets about recruiting him to the Brotherhood. That his motives might be suspect is evident from the beginning, when he asks the invisible man, "How would you like to be the new Booker T. Washington?" (Washington was viewed negatively as an accommodationist by many blacks) and warns him, "You mustn't waste your emotions on individuals, they don't count." Brother Jack turns out to be the author of an anonymous threat mailed to the invisible man.

Mr. Kimbro

The invisible man's first supervisor at Liberty Paints.

Mr. Norton

A white philanthropist and trustee of the college attended by the invisible man, Mr. Norton describes himself as "a trustee of consciousness" and believes that the students of the college are his "fate." He calls his "real life's work ... my firsthand organizing of human life." A romantic about race, he insists on being taken to the old slave quarters, where he expects to hear a lively folktale but instead is treated to a matter-of-fact account of incest by Jim Trueblood. Norton is the cause of the invisible man's expulsion from the school.

Old Bucket-head

See Dr. A. Herbert Bledsoe

Mary Rambo

Mary Rambo runs a rooming house and takes the invisible man in after finding him ill in the street following his stay in the factory hospital. The only person to treat him with genuine affection, Mary is cynical about the big city, and puts her faith in the newcomers from the south: "I'm in New York, but New York ain't in me." The invisible man does not think of Mary as a "'friend'; she was something more—a force, a stable, familiar force like something out of my past which kept me from whirling off into some unknown which I dared not face."

Ras the Exhorter

Modeled on Marcus Garvey, though not a caricature of him. Ras is a flamboyant West African nationalist who preaches black pride, a return to Mother Africa, and a willingness to die for one's principles. Ras and the Brotherhood are engaged in a perpetual turf war, and Ras repeatedly exhorts the black members of the Brotherhood to remember their history. He says to Brother Tod Clifton: "You *my* brother, mahn. Brothers are the same color; how the hell you call these white men *brother?*... Brothers the same color. We sons of Mama Africa, you done forgot? You black, BLACK! ... You African. AFRICAN!"

Rinehart

A mysterious figure who signs himself a "Spiritual Technologist." The reader never meets Rinehart, but the invisible man is mistaken for him by so many different people that he ends up putting together a fascinating though confusing composite: "Still, could he be all of them: Rine the runner and Rine the gambler and Rine the briber and Rine the lover and Rinehart the Reverend? Could he himself be both rind and heart? What is real anyway? ... Perhaps the truth was always a lie." It is in trying to figure out Rinehart that the invisible man begins to see both how complex reality is and that it is possible to live with contradictions.

Sybil

Wife of a member of the Brotherhood with whom the invisible man has a brief liaison in the hope of gaining inside information on the organization.

Brother Tarp

An old but ideologically vigorous member of the Brotherhood. "He can be depended upon in the most precarious circumstance," Brother Jack tells the invisible man. Brother Tarp hangs on the invisible man's office wall a picture of Frederick Douglass, which reminds him of his grandfather. Unlike the invisible man, who left the south more or less voluntarily, Brother Tarp was forced to escape to the north after spending nineteen years on a chain gang because "I said no to a man who wanted to take something from me." He gives the invisible man a link from his ankle iron as a keepsake.

Jim Trueblood

Once respected as a hard worker and a lively storyteller, Jim Trueblood is a black sharecropper who has since shamed the black community and who shocks Mr. Norton with his matter-of-fact account of incest with his daughter. Despite the awfulness of his crime, Trueblood's refusal to stint on the details or to make excuses for himself reveals a basic integrity that is reflected in his name, and the invisible man listens to him with a mixture of horror and admiration.

Veteran at the Golden Day

A skilled doctor who served in France and on his return to the States is run out of town and ends up in the local mental hospital. He attends to Mr. Norton after his heart attack at the Golden Day. The invisible man is impressed with the bold way the vet talks to the white trustee. The vet is the first person to grasp the invisible man's dilemma: "You cannot see or hear or smell the truth of what you see."

Peter Wheatstraw

A kindly rubbish man the invisible man meets in the streets of Harlem singing the blues and who makes him think nostalgically of home.

Brother Wrestrum

A troublemaker, jealous of the invisible man. He makes a false accusation that indirectly results in the protagonist's being taken out of Harlem and sent downtown.

Identity

In *Invisible Man*, an unnamed protagonist sets out on a journey of self-discovery that takes him from the rural south to Harlem. Learning who he is means realizing that he is invisible to the white world, but by the end of his journey the hero has the moral fiber to live with such contradictions. The overwhelming theme of the novel is that of identity. While the novel has to do with questions of race and prejudice, most critics agree that these ideas are subsumed under the broader questions of who we think we are, and the relationship between identity and personal responsibility. The invisible man's moment of self-recognition occurs almost simultaneously with his realization that the white world does not see him, but Ellison seems to be saying, "Well, don't worry about that." Until the invisible man can see himself, he can only be passive, "outside of history." At the beginning of the novel, even Jim Trueblood has a stronger sense of himself than does the hero: "and while I'm singen' them blues I makes up my mind that I ain't nobody but myself and ain't nothin' I can do but let whatever is gonna happen, happen." In fact, everybody but the invisible man seems to be aware of his problem. The vet at The Golden Day sees it, remarking to Mr. Norton: "Already he is—well, bless my soul! Behold! a walking zombie! Already he's learned to repress not only his emotions but his humanity. He's invisible, a walking personification of the Negative, the most perfect achievement of your dreams, sir! The mechanical man!" And Mr. Bledsoe, the college president, tells the hero, "You're nobody, son. You don't exist—can't you see that?" Ironically, when the invisible man offers to prove his identity to the son of Mr. Emerson, a white trustee, the son answers him in the careless manner of someone for whom identity has never been a question, "Identity! My God! Who has any identity any more anyway?" When the invisible man joins the Brotherhood, Brother Jack gives him a "new identity."

Though he constantly stumbles, every misstep seems to bring the hero a little closer to solving the puzzle of who he is. For example, after the operation at the hospital, when a doctor holds up a sign that reads "WHO WAS BUCKEYE THE RABBIT?", the invisible man begins thinking about his identity. And in the wake of Brother Clifton's murder, he remembers past humiliations and sees that they have defined him.

Individualism

Another theme that pervades the novel is that of individuality. Although he may be uncertain of his identity, the invisible man has never quite lost the sense that he is an individual. One of the superficial arguments he uses for leaving Mary Rambo without saying goodbye to her is that people like her "usually think in terms of 'we' while I have always tended to think in terms of 'me'—and that has caused some friction, even with my own family." He rationalizes the Brotherhood's emphasis on the group by deluding himself into thinking that it is a "bigger 'we.'" But though he tries, the invisible man cannot fully suppress his individuality, which continues to intrude on his consciousness. After his first official speech to the Brotherhood, he remembers unaccountably the words of Woodridge, a lecturer at the college, who told his students that their task was "that of making ourselves individuals.... We create the race by creating ourselves." At the funeral for Brother Tod Clifton, whose murder is one of several epiphanies, or moments of illumination, in the novel, the invisible man looks out over the people present and sees "not a crowd but the set faces of individual men and women."

Duty and Responsibility

The theme of responsibility has to do with making choices and accepting the consequences of our actions. The invisible man uses the term at several reprises, but it is only toward the end of his adventures that he is able to match the word with its true meaning. In the course of the "battle royal," he uses the words "social responsibility" to impress the Board of Education, because "whenever I uttered a word of three or more syllables a group of voices would yell for me to repeat it." When he cannot get Dr. Bledsoe to see that what has happened to Dr.

Norton is not his fault, the hero believes that by taking "responsibility" for the mishap he will be able to get on with his career. But what he means by taking responsibility is smoothing things over, and he cannot control the result. As he moves from one troubling experience to another, however, a growing maturity is evident, and people come to depend on him. When Brother Jack asks him by what authority he organized the rally for the people following Brother Tod Clifton's funeral, the invisible man tells him it was on his "personal responsibility," and offers a coolly reasoned defense. At the end of the novel, when he is about to leave his hole, he talks about the "possibility of action" and explains that even an "invisible man has a socially responsible role to play," echoing with mild irony the phrase he once used without thinking.

Blindness

Blindness as a kind of moral and personal failing is a recurring motif, or theme, in the novel. Whether inflicted by others, as in the "battle royal," where the young men are forcibly blindfolded, or as evidence of confusion, as when the invisible man describes stumbling "in a game of blindman's buff," the idea of blindness is used to multiple effect. The Reverend Homer A. Barbee is literally blind, Brother Jack has a glass eye, white people cannot see the invisible man, and the hero cannot see himself. A variation on the theme is the idea of looking but not seeing, of not *trying* to see, which comes back to the theme of responsibility. Various characters impress on the invisible man the importance of not accepting things as they are. "For God's sake," the vet from The Golden Day tells him, "learn to look beneath the surface. Come out of the fog, young man." And the son of the white trustee Emerson asks him, "Aren't you curious about what lies behind the face of things?"

History and Folklore

In *Invisible Man* history and identity are inextricably bound: we are the sum of our history and our experience. This message is brought home in the novel both overtly—"What is your past and where are you going?" Ras the Exhorter asks an uncomfortable Brother Tod Clifton—and indirectly, as in Mary Rambo's advice to the invisible man that it is the young who will make changes but "something's else, it's the ones from the South that's got to do it, them what knows the fire and ain't forgot how it bums. Up here too many forgits." That is, you are your history, but only if you remember it. An inventory of the sad belongings of the couple the hero finds on the Harlem sidewalk reads like a synopsis of the story of blacks in America, and the power of the associations the objects evoke inspires the invisible man to address a crowd for the first time. Closely related to the theme of history is the motif of folklore as a link to the past, particularly folktales, jazz, and the blues. The simple folk who appear in the book all seem rooted in a way the invisible man and others are not, and have a sureness about them that is reflected in their names:

Jim Trueblood, Mary Rambo, Peter Wheatstraw, even Ras the Exhorter. Likewise, the hero's grandfather has a "stolid black peasant's face." The vet at The Golden Day, who is a mental patient but does not appear to be completely insane, tells Mr. Norton that he had made a mistake in forgetting certain "fundamentals.... Things about life. Such things as most peasants and folk peoples almost always know through experience, though seldom through conscious thought."

Topics for Further Study

- Research some of the major demographic shifts occurring in the world today, and compare the reasons for them with those that motivated the Great Migration North of 1910–1970 in the United States.

- Explore current policies in medical ethics and informed consent and explain how these would affect the circumstances of the kind of operation performed on the invisible man in Ellison's novel.

- Investigate current housing laws regarding the elderly, and explain how the couple who are evicted from their apartment in winter in the novel would be affected by them, and what their options for alternative living arrangements might be.

Style

Point of View

At the outset of *Invisible Man*, the unnamed hero is in transition. He has discovered that he is invisible and has retreated from the world in defiance; but the reader senses that all is not resolved. In the adventure that the invisible man proceeds to relate in the first person ("I"), his voice changes over time from that of a naive young man, to someone who is clearly more responsible though still confused, to a person willing to deal with the world whatever the risks. The novel is framed by a Prologue and Epilogue. The story opens in the present, switches to flashback, and then returns to the present, but a step forward from the Prologue.Writing down the story has helped the hero to make up his mind about things. Leonard J. Deutsch attributes the complexity of the novel in part to this juxtaposition of perspectives of the "I" of the naive boy and the "I" of the older, wiser narrator. Anthony West, on the other hand, writing in *The New Yorker*, called the Prologue and the Epilogue "intolerably arty ... the two worst pieces of writing in the work."

Setting

Invisible Man is set in an indeterminate time frame sometime between the 1930s and 1950s. The protagonist's adventures take him from an unnamed southern town to New York City, mirroring the migration during the period of the novel of over a quarter of a million African Americans from the rural south to the urban north in search of jobs. The novel opens on the campus of a southern black college whose buildings and environs are repeatedly described in honeyed terms. Nevertheless, in retrospect the hero remembers it also as a flower-studded wasteland maintained by the money of white philanthropists blind to the surrounding poverty. The action then moves to Harlem, a part of New York City associated with several political and cultural elements of importance in the novel: the active recruiting of black intellectuals by the Communist party in the United States, the rise of black nationalism, and the golden age of jazz.

Symbol

Invisible Man is rich with symbols that have given critics fertile ground for interpretation. For example, the "battle royal" that opens the book represents the novel in a nutshell and serves as a microcosmic portrayal of race relations in a socially segregated society. The narrator will clutch to him the briefcase the Board of Education awards him throughout his adventures, though he will burn its contents—which symbolize his middle-class aspirations—at the end. Ellison gives his characters names that often suggest something about their personalities, for example, Dr. Bledsoe, Jim Trueblood, Brother Wrestrum, or equally significant, as in the case of the protagonist, he does not name them at all. Songs figure significantly in the novel. In the prologue, for instance, the hero remembers the words to a Louis Armstrong song, "What did I do *To be so black* And blue?" and at the end of the catastrophic visit to the slave quarters, which will result in the hero's expulsion from college, the children are singing "London Bridge Is Falling Down." The lobotomy-like operation undertaken to make the hero more amiable backfires and instead brings him somewhat to himself, constituting a symbolic rebirth.

Literary Styles

The many stylistic elements used in *Invisible Man* are part of what make it such a literary tour de force. Warren French, for example, has described the formal organization of the narrative as "a series of nested boxes that an individual, trapped in the constricting center, seeks to escape." Several critics cite the use of varied literary styles, from the naturalism of the events at the college campus, to the expressionism, or subjective emotions, of the hero's time with the Brotherhood, to the surrealism that characterizes the riot at the end of the novel. *Invisible Man* can be classed as a *bildungsroman*, or novel of education, similar to Voltaire's *Candide*, in which the hero moves from innocence to experience. It has also been called picaresque because of the episodic nature of the hero's adventures, but this term implies a shallowness that the invisible man is finally able to overcome.

Comedy and irony are used to good effect in both the episode with Jim Trueblood and the scene at The Golden Day. But most important, Ellison drew on the knowledge of African American folklore he acquired in his days with the Federal Writers Project, and the influence of that tradition, particularly jazz and the blues, is inextricably woven into the thought and speech of the characters. The Reverend Homer A. Barbee's address, for example, is alive with gospel rhythms: "'But she knew, she knew! She knew the fire! She knew the fire! She knew the fire that burned without consuming! My God, yes!'"

The Great Migration

The civil rights movement of the 1950s and 1960s had its genesis in the Great Migration, the move north of 6.5 million black Americans from the rural South. This created large black communities like New York's Harlem and Chicago's South Side. In the early 1900s, black migration increased dramatically with the beginning of World War I in 1914, in response to the demand for factory workers in the north. While the move did not bring social justice to blacks, it did provide some social, financial, and political benefits, and it established the issue of race in the national consciousness. Both Ralph Ellison and his protagonist, like so many before them, made the journey north. When the invisible man tells the vet from The Golden Day that he's going to New York, the vet answers, "New York! That's not a place, it's a dream. When I was your age it was Chicago. Now all the little black boys run away to New York."

Compare & Contrast

- **1930s:** Following an active policy of inclusion, the Communist party recruits many black leaders and thinkers.

1952: A "witch-hunt" for communists begun by U.S. Senator Joseph McCarthy continues through the early 1950s and ruins many careers.

Today: The 1980s see the collapse of communism in Eastern Europe. In America, politics is increasingly middle-of-the-road. American communists are a small fringe group.

- **1930s:** The U.S. labor movement gains support under the New Deal, but prejudice against African Americans is widespread.

  1952: Union membership peaks in 1945 at 35.5% of the non-agricultural workforce and is still strong in the 1950s.

  Today: Unions are fully integrated. But membership is at an all-time low, and unions are forced to compromise on wages and benefits to preserve jobs.

- **1930s:** Brain surgery to correct the behavior of mentally ill patients, or lobotomy, is widely practiced between 1936 and 1956.

  1952: Lobotomy is largely abandoned in favor of alternative treatments including tranquilizers and psychotherapy.

Today: Psychoactive drugs have become the first line of treatment for mental illness, and a de-emphasis of institutional care and the closing of mental hospitals have produced increased homelessness.

- **1930s:** Big bands in the swing era give way to bebop, the basis for modern jazz, which arises in Kansas City and Harlem. Major influences are Charlie Parker, Dizzy Gillespie, and Thelonius Monk.
  1952: Progressive, or cool, jazz, with less convoluted melodic lines, begins in New York City in the late 1940s and early 1950s. Lester Young and Miles Davis are major figures in the movement, which is better received critically than bebop.
  Today: After a period of several decades of experimentation, including a style called fusion, jazz settles into a revivalist phase. Popular artists include Wynton and Branford Marsalis, David Murray, and John Carter.

Northern black factory workers could expect to make two to ten times as much as their southern counterparts, and thus newly arrived blacks from the south had an uneasy relationship with organized white labor. Their reluctance to jeopardize their access to the industrial job market by taking part in labor agitation was exploited by their employers to frustrate unions who hired black laborers to replace strikers. It was already clear by the 1930s that America's labor movement could only survive through integration, and between 1935 and the end of World War II, 500,000 blacks joined the Congress of Industrial Organizations (CIO). But white opposition to bringing blacks into the unions persisted up to the time Ellison wrote *Invisible Man.* At Liberty Paints an office boy tells the invisible man, "The wise guys firing the regular guys and putting on you colored college boys. Pretty smart. That way they don't have to pay union wages." And when Lucius Brockway mistakenly thinks the invisible man has gone to a labor meeting, he fairly explodes. "'That damn union,' he cried, almost in tears. 'That damn union! They after my job! For one of us to join one of them damn unions is like we was to bite the hand of the man who taught us to bathe in the bathtub!'"

American communists strongly advocated racial tolerance, thereby winning the support of black leaders and intellectuals, particularly during the Depression. Like Richard Wright, Ellison leaned on the party for financial support and because it offered him a way of getting published. Nevertheless, Ellison objected to what he considered to be a kind of thought control, and he never became a party member. During World War II, when the party advised against pushing issues of racial segregation in the U.S. armed forces, Ellison became disillusioned. In *Invisible Man*, the hero returns from an absence only to discover that "there had been, to my surprise, a switch in emphasis from local issues to those more national and international in scope, and it was felt for the moment the interests of Harlem were not of first importance."

Nationhood and Civil Rights

In 1916, Marcus Garvey came to the United States from Jamaica and founded the Universal Negro Improvement Association (UNIA). Like Ras the Exhorter in *Invisible Man*, Garvey was an ardent and flamboyant nationalist, and he electrified Harlem with his message of black pride and selfdetermination through the recolonization of Africa. But Garvey's arguments for racial separation were at odds with the integrationist efforts of communists, and the schism between the two groups would outlast Garvey's political demise in 1921. Another significant black nationalist figure of the 1930s was Sufi Abdul Mohammed; elements of his colorful personality turn up in *Invisible Man* in both Ras the Exhorter and Rinehart, the mysterious numbers runner and preacher.

Some 400,000 black soldiers served in World War I, but they found that their devotion did not translate into respect abroad during the war or at home after it. Once overseas, blacks were relegated to menial tasks, were passed over for combat duty, and were subjected to continual harassment by whites. The society to which they returned was even more conservative on issues of race than the one they had left. The black press, particular W. E. B. Du Bois's influential magazine *The Crisis*, was loud in its condemnation of reports of discriminatory treatment made by returning black soldiers. The outrage felt by black veterans is described in an incident in *Invisible Man*, where a group of black World War I veterans cause a disturbance at a whorehouse and bar called The Golden Day. One veteran describes how he had served as a surgeon in France under the Army Medical Corps but was chased out of town on his return to America.

The prospect of a new draft in the wake of the eruption of conflict in Europe again in 1939 led to civil rights protests in the early 1940s and violent racial incidents between white southerners and black northerners at military bases across the United States. The issue was responsible for the Harlem riot of 1943. The climax of *Invisible Man* is a riot in Harlem allegedly instigated by the Brotherhood; the event is based in part on a riot that occurred there in 1935, which some commentators blamed on communist agitators.

Critical Overview

Invisible Man was published to instant acclaim, though its complexity did not necessarily make it an easy read. Writing in *Commentary* in 1952, Saul Bellow called it "a book of the very first order, a superb book," praising in particular the episode in which Jim Trueblood tells his tale of incent to Mr. Norton. "One is accustomed to expect excellent novels about boys, but a modern novel about men is exceedingly rare." Anthony West wrote in *The New Yorker* that *Invisible Man* was "an exceptionally good book and in parts an extremely funny one" and praised its "robust courage," though he recommended skipping the Prologue and Epilogue and "certain expressionist passages conveniently printed in italics." Like Bellow, West congratulated Ellison on having written a book "about being colored in a white society [that] yet manages not to be a grievance book" and noted Ellison's "real satirical gift for handling ideas at the level of low comedy." In his study *Native Sons*, Edward Margolies noted the importance of jazz and the blues to the narrative and commented that what Ellison "seems to be saying [is] that if men recognize first that existence is purposeless, they may then be able to perceive the possibility of shaping their existence in some kind of viable form —in much the same manner as the blues artist gives form to his senseless pain and suffering." However, Margolies bemoaned the thematic weakness of the novel, which is that "Ellison's hero simply has nowhere to go once he tells us he is invisible." In a 1963 article in *Dissent*, Irving Howe called the novel a brilliant though flawed achievement. "No white man could have written it, since no white man could know with such intimacy the life of the Negroes from the inside; yet Ellison writes with an ease and humor which are now and again simply miraculous."

The style of the novel has occasionally been criticized as excessive—Howe found Ellison "literary to a fault"—but even the novel's critics found much to praise in the symbolism, style, and narrative structure. Opinion was divided over the section dealing with the Brotherhood. West called it "perhaps the best description of rank-and-file Communist Party activity that has yet appeared in an American novel," but Bellow found it less than convincing, and Howe wrote that "Ellison makes his Stalinist figures so vicious and stupid that one cannot understand how they could ever have attracted him or any other Negro."

The biggest controversy over the book has always had to do with whether or not it was intended for a universal audience. Bellow praised Ellison for not having "adopted a minority tone. If he had done so, he would have failed to establish a true middle-of-consciousness for everyone." Howe felt rather that "even Ellison cannot help being caught up with the idea of the Negro, ... for plight and protest are inseparable from that experience," though he did not say whether this was good or bad.

Warren French asserts in *Reference Guide to American Fiction* that the book has frequently been misread: it is neither unique to the black experience nor "picaresque," but both broader and more sophisticated. David Littlejohn straddled the debate, called *Invisible Man* "essentially a Negro's novel … written entirely out of a Negro's experience, … [b]ut it is not a 'Negro novel.'… It is his story, really, not the race's, not the war's, except insofar as he is of the race and in the war." Black nationalists argued that Ellison was not stringent enough, and John Oliver Killens and Amiri Baraka were particularly vocal critics. Ellison's defense was that he had never been a propagandist.

In 1953 *Invisible Man* was awarded the National Book Award for fiction. But controversy over what it meant and to whom continued. In his preface to the 1981 commnemorative edition of the novel, Charles Johnson, whose *Middle Passage* won the National Book Award in 1990, remembers a time in the 1960s when "both Ellison and poet Robert Hayden were snubbed by those under the spell of black cultural nationalism, and when so many black critics denied the idea of 'universality' in literature and life." This attitude was largely reversed during the 1970s when white critics tired of waiting for Ellison's hypothetical second novel and black readers began to be more appreciative of the book's portrayal of black experience. Whatever the nature of the critical debate, *Invisible Man* has proved its staying power. Leonard Deutsch wrote that for all its brutal realism and cynicism, *Invisible Man* "is basically a comic and celebratory work, for the hero is ultimately better off at the end: he has become the shaping artist of his tale."

Sources

Saul Bellow, "Man Underground," in *Commentary*, June, 1952, pp. 608–10.

Leonard J. Deutsch, "Ralph Ellison," in *Dictionary of Literary Biography, Volume 2: American Novelists since World War II* edited by Jeffrey Helterman and Richard Layman, Gale Research, 1978, pp. 136–40.

Warren French, "Invisible Man," in *Reference Guide to American Literature*, 3rd edition, St. James Press, 1994, pp. 993–94.

Irving Howe, "Black Boys and Native Sons," in *Dissent*, Autumn, 1963.

Charles Johnson, "The Singular Vision of Ralph Ellison," preface to *Invisible Man*, Modern Library, 1994, pp. vii-xii.

David Littlejohn, *inBlack on White: A Critical Survey of Writing by American Negroes*, Viking, pp. 110–119.

Edward Margolies, "History as Blues: Ralph Ellison's 'Invisible Man,' " in his *Native Sons: A Critical Study of Twentieth-Century Negro American Authors*, Lippincott, 1968, pp. 127–48.

Anthony West, "Black Man's Burden," in *The New Yorker*, Volume 28, No. 15, May 31, 1952, pp. 93–96.

For Further Study

Kimberly W. Benston, editor, *Speaking for You: The Vision of Ralph Ellison*, Howard University Press, 1987.

> A wide-ranging collection of essays on Ellison's fiction and nonfiction as well as interviews with Ellison and poems written in his honor.

Ralph Ellison, *The Collected Essays of Ralph Ellison*, edited by John F. Callahan, Modern Library, 1995.

> A recent collection of all of Ellison's essays, reviews, and interviews, some previously unpublished. Includes the complete text of Ellison's two published collections, *Shadow and Act* and *Going to the Territory*, as well as his introduction to the Thirtieth Anniversary Edition of *Invisible Man.*

Ralph Ellison, *Conversations with Ralph Ellison*, edited by Maryemma Graham and Amritjit Singh, University Press of Mississippi, 1995.

> A collection of interviews with Ellison including considerable commentary on *Invisible Man.*

John Hersey, editor, *Ralph Ellison: A Collection of Critical Essays*, Prentice-Hall, 1974.

A collection of early reviews, an interview with Ellison, and several important essays on *Invisible Man*.

Alan Nadel, *Invisible Criticism: Ralph Ellison and the American Canon*, University of Iowa Press, 1988.

Nadel reads Ellison's novel as a commentary on the formation of the American literary canon through its allusions to canonical figures such as Emerson, Melville, and Twain.

Robert G. O'Meally, *The Craft of Ralph Ellison*, Harvard University Press, 1980.

An important critical study of Ellison's life and his writing, with particular attention to Ellison's characters and the "fictional world" they inhabit.

Robert G. O'Meally, editor, *New Essays on Invisible Man*, Cambridge University Press, 1988.

A collection of five recent essays on *Invisible Man* with an historical overview in O'Meally's Introduction.

Susan Resneck Parr and Pancho Savery, *Approaches to Teaching Ellison's Invisible Man*, Modern Language Association, 1980.

Though intended primarily for teachers, this collection of brief essays also offers the first-time reader several productive avenues into Ellison's novel.

David Remnick, "VisibleMan," in *The New Yorker*, March 14, 1994, pp. 34-38.

> Published just one month before Ellison's death, this essay discusses the importance of his writings to discussions of race in America since the 1960s.

Eric J. Sundquist, editor, *Cultural Contexts for Ralph Ellison's Invisible Man*, Bedford, 1995.

> This useful collection "illuminates and contextualizes" Ellison's novel by gathering various historical and cultural documents, including speeches, essays, songs, and folktales.

Joseph F. Trimmer, editor, *A Casebook on Ralph Ellison's Invisible Man*, Thomas Y. Crowell, 1972.

> A collection of essays that places Ellison in the context of both a "racial heritage" and an "artistic heritage" and concludes with a listing of "possible discussion questions or research topics."

Lightning Source UK Ltd.
Milton Keynes UK
UKHW022059120721
387052UK00007B/1191